The Nature Kid's Guide to

MICE

DAVID ANDERSON

LP Media Inc. Publishing
Text copyright © 2026 by LP Media Inc.
All rights reserved.

For information address LP Media Inc. Publishing,
30012 Variolite St NW, Princeton MN 55371
www.lpmedia.org

Publication Data

Mice
The Nature Kid's Guide to Mice — First edition.

Summary: "Learn all about Mice, the Nature Kid Way"
— Provided by publisher.

ISBN: 979-8-89818-160-4

[1. Mice – Non-Fiction] I. Title.

Title: The Nature Kid's Guide to Mice

CONTENTS

MIGHTY MICE

Pitter, patter! A brave mouse scurries across the forest floor.

Mice can live almost anywhere! But they need a few things to survive. They need shelter, food, and water nearby.

Some mice like warm, dry fields. They build nests in tall grain. Other mice live in cool, damp forests. They hide under fallen leaves and logs.

Mice are great at hiding. Thick grass keeps them out of sight. Piles of rocks work well too. They can squeeze into tiny spaces to escape danger.

Some mice dig burrows three feet deep! These tunnels have rooms for sleeping and storing food.

MICE EVERYWHERE

Crack! A tiny mouse nibbles through a seed shell. Its whiskers twitch.

Mice live all over the world. They live on every continent except Antarctica. House mice first came from Asia long ago. Now they live wherever people live.

Deer mice are common in North America. They live from Canada to Mexico. Wood mice are found across Europe.

African pygmy mice live in sub-Saharan Africa. Harvest mice make homes in Europe and Asia.

House mice traveled on ships with explorers. They sailed to new lands around the world!

MINI MICE

Sip! A deer mouse drinks from a single tiny dewdrop.

Mice are very small animals. Most mice have a body that is 3 to 4 inches long. That is about as long as your finger!

A house mouse weighs less than one ounce. That is about the same as four nickels! You can easily hold a mouse in one hand.

A mouse is much smaller than a hamster or a rat.

The pygmy mouse is the smallest mouse. It weighs about 2 grams, lighter than a penny!

TINY TAILS

A mouse's tail has thin hair but no fur. It helps keep the mouse cool in hot weather!

Scurry! A little mouse runs up to drink from a tiny puddle.

Mice have bodies built for survival. Their soft fur keeps them warm and dry. It can be brown, gray, white, or black.

Mouse paws are super cool. Each paw has tiny claws for gripping. These claws help mice climb walls and ropes.

Mice have long, thin tails. The tail helps them balance when they run.

Their large ears can turn to catch sounds.

Mice have sharp front teeth that never stop growing. They must chew to keep them short.

SUPER SNIFFERS

Quiet! A tiny mouse freezes. Its whiskers sense danger.

Mice have a super sense of smell. They can smell things that humans cannot. A mouse uses this power to find food in the dark.

Mice also hear high-pitched sounds that humans cannot hear. In fact they hear noises almost five times better than humans do!

Their long whiskers aren't just to look cool either. They help mice feel their way through dark tunnels safely.

Mice can smell a tiny crumb of food from across a room, even in total darkness!

HIDE WELL

Peek! A tiny house mouse squeezes through a hole in the wall.

Mice have special tricks that keep them safe from danger. Their fur helps them hide. Brown and gray fur blends with dirt and rocks. This is called **camouflage**.

Mice can squeeze through holes as small as a dime. They slip into tiny cracks and gaps. These small spaces keep them safe from **predators**.

Mice also stay very still when danger is near. Staying hidden keeps mice safe from hungry animals.

DID YOU KNOW?

Mice do not change color in winter, but animals like weasels and snowshoe hares do.

MUNCHING MICE

Chomp! Tiny teeth work through a crunchy grain. A hungry mouse eats.

Mice eat many kinds of food. Seeds and grains are their favorites. They also munch on fruits, nuts, and berries.

Mice eat insects and worms too. Some mice nibble on plants and roots. They will try almost any food they find.

A mouse eats about 3 to 5 grams of food each day. That is about 1/5 their bodyweight. That's like if you ate 20 hamburgers every day!

Mice can chew through wood, plastic, and even concrete!

SQUEAKY SPEAK

FUN FACT!
Mice thump their front paws on the ground to warn other mice that danger is close!

Squeak! A wood mouse stops and listens. Her babies are calling her!

Mice talk to each other with squeaks and chirps. Some sounds are so high that people cannot hear them. These special sounds are called **ultrasonic** calls.

Mice also use their bodies to communicate. A scared mouse stands very still, while an angry mouse may show its teeth.

Scent is important for mouse talk too. Mice leave smell marks with their urine. These marks help tell other mice who lives nearby. Mother mice also use smell to recognize their babies.

WATCH OUT

Hiss! A rattlesnake slithers through the tall grass. It is hunting for mice.

Many animals hunt mice. Owls, hawks, and eagles catch mice from the sky. Their sharp eyes spot tiny mice on the ground.

Snakes hunt mice too. They can follow mice into **burrows** and tunnels. Foxes and coyotes dig mice out of their hiding spots.

Cats, weasels, and even large fish eat mice. With so many predators, mice must always stay alert.

Barn owls can catch mice in total darkness. They hunt using only sound.

QUICK ESCAPE

Whoosh! A wood mouse jumps through a gap and vanishes into the tall grass.

Mice are experts at escaping danger. They can squeeze through tiny holes and cracks. Their flexible bodies flatten to fit into tiny spaces.

When scared, mice will run in zigzag patterns. This confuses predators trying to catch them.

Mice can also jump up to 12 inches high. This helps them leap away from danger in a split second!

A mouse can fall from a height of 12 feet and land without getting hurt. Their tiny bodies are so light they barely feel the drop!

23

SCURRY FAST

24

Jump! A mouse leaps through the grass. She's heading back to her nest.

Mice are fast runners. They can sprint up to 8 miles per hour. Their small legs help them move very quickly.

Mice are great climbers too. They climb up walls and rough surfaces that many animals would slip off of. Their sharp claws help them grip tightly.

Mice can also swim. They paddle with their tiny paws and use their tail to steer through the water. If a flood comes, some mice will swim for up to three days without stopping!

NIGHT LIFE

Hoot! A tiny deer mouse scurries out to play as the sun sets.

Mice are **nocturnal**. This means they are active at night. They sleep during the day in cozy nests.

When darkness comes, mice wake up. They spend hours looking for food. They also explore new places and groom their fur.

Mice have poor eyesight. But their large eyes help them see in dim light. They also use their whiskers and smell to find their way in the dark.

Mice stay close to home, usually traveling only 10 to 30 feet from their nest to find food.

MOUSE MOBS

Splash! Tiny mice scurry across the wet morning grass.

Mice live in groups called colonies. Many mice share nests and food together.

Mice are social animals. They groom each other and sleep in piles. This keeps them warm and safe.

A mouse group has a dominant male leader. The whole group works together. They tell each other where to find food. They warn each other about danger.

Mice remember their friends by smell. Each mouse has its own unique scent, like a smelly fingerprint!

FINDING FRIENDS

Cute! Two mice meet by the pond and touch noses.

Mice can have babies all year long. They do not wait for a special season. This helps mouse populations grow quickly.

To find a mate, male mice make ultrasonic sounds. These sounds are too high for humans to hear, but female mice hear them well.

Female mice can have babies when they are just six weeks old. A mother can have a new litter every three weeks!

Male mice chase and sniff females to impress them. They run and follow the females around!

PINK PUPS

DID YOU KNOW?

A mother mouse uses smell to tell her babies from one another, even in a litter of twelve babies!

Tiny pink mice wiggle in their cozy nest. No fur yet!

Baby mice are called pups or pinkies. They are born with no fur. Their skin is pink and see-through. You can almost see inside them!

But by the time they are one week old, fuzzy fur starts to grow. By two weeks old they have a full coat!

Newborn pups are very small. They weigh less than a paperclip. Their eyes and ears are closed tight, so they cannot see or hear yet.

Most litters have six to eight pups. Some litters have even more. That is a lot of tiny babies in one nest!

MOM KNOWS

DID YOU KNOW?
Mother mice build nests from soft grass, paper, and bits of cloth.

34

Push! A mother mouse nudges her babies into the nest.

Mother mice nurse their babies with milk and keep them warm in the nest. Sometimes other females or even the father help watch over the pups.

Mouse pups grow quickly. Their eyes open after about two weeks. They can also hear sounds by this age.

Mothers teach pups how to find food. Young mice follow their mom around and learn what is safe to eat. Pups leave the nest at three weeks old.

By six weeks old, pups have become full-grown adult mice!

MARVELOUS MICE

Crunch! A wood mouse nibbles seeds in a cozy nest of straw.

Mice are amazing learners. Scientists use them to study how brains work. Mice can even learn their names and will come when called!

Mice have helped people make important medicines. They help doctors find cures for diseases.

Scientists once even taught mice to play simple video games using a tiny joystick. The mice got better the more they played!

Mice have incredible memories. Scientists have watched mice learn a maze and remember every twist and turn, even weeks later!

HAPPY HOMES

Sip! A tiny pet mouse drinks from its bowl. Home sweet home!

Mice can make great pets, but providing good care for them is very important.

Pet mice need fresh water every day. They drink from small bottles or bowls. They also need mouse food from the pet store.

They need a clean cage. It must be cleaned once a week. They need new soft bedding for them to nest in.

Pet mice can learn tricks. They can spin in circles and jump through tiny hoops for treats!

GLOSSARY

burrows
Underground tunnels that animals dig to live in.

camouflage
Colors or patterns that help an animal hide by blending in with its surroundings.

predators
Animals that hunt and eat other animals.

ultrasonic
Sounds that are so high that people cannot hear them.

nocturnal
Active at night and sleeping during the day.

www.ingramcontent.com/pod-product-compliance
Lightning Source LLC
Chambersburg PA
CBHW042126150726

48005CB00029B/415